Trust in the "Yord"

Hunter's Story

Pam Long

Trust in the "Yord"

Hunter's Story

Pam Long

Library of Congress Cataloging-in-Publication Data
Long, Pam
Christian Non-Fiction/Pam Long—1st ed.
p. cm.

"A Regal Ink Press publication"

ISBN 978-0-9842964-4-6

Design and Layout by Stephen Cassar
Typeset in Schneidler Lt Bt and Segoe UI Light
Designed and Printed in the United States of America

because of Hunter

2 Corinthians 1:3-4

foreword

Finding "heroes" today is no easy matter. Often we look for the wrong things in the wrong people. We neglect some of the most critical aspects… things like character, faith, authenticity or joy. Pam and Eldon are two of mine. Let me tell you why.

They are an amazing family – the whole clan. I've gotten to know them all; their heart for God and for others around them is genuine and overflowing. They reach out to so many as they go through life on a daily basis. I am one of those lucky recipients. As a pastoral staff member, I have known the Long family for fifteen years. I remember visiting Chris & Greta in the hospital when Hunter was born, and sadly, I was part of the memorial celebration at the end of his life.

I was there the evening of September 26th, 2004. I had a front row seat to the unfolding of those events, as well as the time since. I arrived at their home shortly after the search and rescue teams, I was with them when they were given the worst of news and I was in the home in the days afterward. So much of that night has remained vivid and fixed in my mind, even after all these years.

I share this for two reasons. First, the events and Pam & Eldon's response have impacted me. Second, I want to authenticate everything shared to be true. I will never forget Eldon taking Chris by the head and speaking bold truth to him on the news of Hunter's death. Eldon drove a spiritual stake in the ground and, I believe, set the course for their grief journey to go forward. While not an easy path, Pam and Eldon never wavered in their trust in Jesus or the joy found in Him.

I believe their story is, in part, to help others. Why wouldn't it be? That's been the whole of their entire lives and I don't think the Lord (or they) would suddenly expect anything different now.

We need heroes, especially ones who have journeyed bravely and survived! When Pam and Eldon speak, I pay attention. If you have found yourself in a similar place, I would encourage you to do the same.

John Marquette, Community Pastor
Fellowship Bible Church of NWA

contents

introduction

As much as we hate to admit it, we will experience the pain of a loss in our lives at some point. That is not a suggestion or a suspicion – it's a cold, hard fact. And, even though we all experience some sort of loss, the pain of that loss won't be the same for everyone because there are definitely different kinds of losses. There are also different intensities of pain resulting from those losses. There is the loss of a job, the loss of a home or place to live, even the loss of a relationship or friendship of many years. Any of these can be heart-wrenching and cause us enormous discomfort and confusion, but the pain of loss through death is what this book is about: the pain of grief.

Webster's New World Dictionary defines the word *grief* as "intense emotional suffering caused as by a loss." I know what you're thinking, "ANOTHER book on grief?" Sadly, it's true that there are countless books available on the subject. It wasn't my intention to write a book on grief but to just write about my precious grandson, Hunter, and the story of his very short life. The two became one.

Death brings grief, and the levels of pain are varied, depending upon the nature of the relationship between the surviving person and the deceased.

You may have experienced a level of grief as a result of the death of a person that you didn't know personally, sometimes a prominent person. Do you remember how people mourned the deaths of JFK and Martin Luther King, Jr.? For those of you from a younger generation, you may recall the grief expressed at the passing of Mother Teresa or of Princess Diana of Wales. Likewise, the terrible loss of life that occurred on 9/11 or in Haiti's earthquake evoked grief worldwide.

Death touches us all in some form or fashion but it's the grief associated with it that is the hardest to deal with. I lost grandparents that were elderly and very ill, a high school friend killed in Vietnam and several friends lost to health issues or automobile wrecks. Those were all very hard, but it was the loss of my only grandson that plunged me into grief like I had never experienced before.

It was the kind of grief that tore at my very being, racked my body with real physical pain and made me believe I might never recover. That was certainly how I felt the minute I realized Hunter was gone. It was a loss I wasn't ready to deal with and truthfully, never expected to.

Someone may have given you this book or you may have purchased it yourself. Regardless of how you came to have it, I don't think it was by accident, because I don't believe in accidents anymore. It's my prayer that, after reading Hunter's story, you won't believe in accidents either. It is also my prayer that Hunter's story will lead you to hope and answers whereas those may have been missing.

The story of how our family lost Hunter is heart-wrenching, as the death of a child always is.

I realize it has become more than that now and that's why I felt so led to share my experience. I want people to know that there is infinitely more to our lives than the pain of grief, and how important it is to recognize that and work through it. The pain of grief is real but we don't have to *stay* in the depths of grief and despair forever. There is a road out of those depths and there is abundant life on the other side. THERE IS HOPE and I'm living proof of it.

chapter one
The Pain

Hunter McKenzie Long was born on October 20, 2000 to my son, Chris, and daughter-in-law, Greta. He was the most amazing baby we had ever seen and beautiful in every way. My husband, Eldon, and I were experiencing the indescribable joys of first-time grandparent-hood (is that a word?) and we just could not wipe the smiles off our faces. We had laid our hands on Greta's tummy early in her pregnancy and prayed that God would use that precious little baby for great things. Just watching him grow and change every day was amazing to us, and although we had three grown children whom we loved very much, our first grandson was really something special. Our hearts were filled to overflowing.

We lived on eleven acres in a nice combination of city and country in Lowell, Arkansas. The property was ringed by big trees, a large expanse of woods, and plenty of nice open space. Our whole family loves the outdoors and we spent a lot of time outside when the weather permitted – especially in the summertime. There is even a little creek that runs through those trees behind the property line called "Puppy Creek," and we all visited it many times in the thirty-two years we lived there.

Chris and Greta's home was on the very back side of the acreage and Hunter loved exploring every inch of the place. He was a budding outdoorsman for sure. His mom and dad took him canoeing, camping, hiking, biking; he loved being outside. We had a swimming pool in our backyard and the rules about being safe had been drilled into him since he was old enough to stand up and toddle around it. He knew he was never to be at the pool without an adult present or without his life jacket on, and he wasn't. He also knew he was never to leave the yard or be in the road that ran in front of our house and he didn't, even though we lived on a dead end street.

We were a close-knit community and well acquainted with our neighbors. One family in our neighborhood owned a beautiful golden retriever named Buster. Buster never met a stranger and he loved visiting everyone on our street from time to time. He especially liked to play with Hunter and vice versa. They played a lot together and I believe they truly loved each other.

It was late Sunday afternoon on September 26, 2004. Buster and Hunter were playing in the yard with Chris watching them both, occasionally joining in the fun as they all enjoyed the fall afternoon. We were going to cook out hamburgers later that evening and Greta, Eldon and I were in another part of our house, talking and making plans for the meal.

After playing for quite a while outside, Chris told Hunter to go in to our house and wash his hands for supper. He actually walked him to the door and put him inside the house, but Hunter promptly walked through my kitchen, through the open garage door and back outside to play with Buster again. None of us inside ever knew he came in the house at all.

Chris came in a short while later, took a quick look around and immediately asked us where Hunter was. We thought he was with Chris; Chris thought he was with us. If you've ever had a child you couldn't find, you know that feeling. Your heart swells into your throat and begins beating wildly; your head pounds and you have a hard time breathing. Everything after that played out like a really bad dream.

As we began looking for him I just kept telling myself, "he'll show up. We'll find him. It's ok. Don't freak out." I never once thought about what might be happening to him at that very moment. I have to say I was worried but wasn't thinking the worst by any means.

We searched our house from top to bottom, then we raced down to Chris and Greta's and searched their house. We called for Hunter until we were all hoarse but he was nowhere to be found. My heart stuck in my throat when I heard Eldon tell Chris it was time to call 911 and my son immediately made the call.

After the police and the emergency vehicles arrived, I felt a little better somehow, thinking that Hunter would see all the vehicles and it would be just a matter of minutes until he came walking up into the yard. The police set up a command post in the field across the road from our house. As darkness fell, big floodlights illuminated the area and I watched the groups of searchers as they received their assignments. I found out later that there were people from all over Benton County that answered the call that night to come and help search for our lost little boy: the Benton County Sheriff's department, off-duty police and firemen, not to mention our whole city police and fire/rescue departments. They all responded so quickly. I just knew they would find him hiding somewhere in a place we had forgotten to look. They didn't.

One officer even brought his search dog and began combing the woods behind our property but we had disturbed the trail by tromping all over and the dog never could pick up Hunter's scent. That's when the reality of the situation really hit me and I began to cry.

The police stopped all cars leaving the area in the event that Hunter had been abducted. I'm not even sure how long the police and other agencies had been there when our neighbor, Linda, drove by and stopped to ask what was going on, since she could see the emergency vehicles and all of us standing around in the yard. Her family owned Buster. I told her Hunter was missing and she told me that she was looking for Buster. I think we both took a small bit of hope from that, believing that Hunter and Buster must surely be together and, when we found one, we would find the other. She told me she'd keep looking for the dog and promised to let us know the minute she found them. She headed back to her house.

By that time we had been joined by our pastor, several neighbors and friends. Someone told me later that a prayer chain had been started by telephone and people were praying that we would find Hunter quickly. We all stood around in the yard, praying and talking quietly, waiting for any word. Eldon got on his bicycle and went door to door in our neighborhood, asking if anyone had seen Hunter or Buster. Chris went back into the woods on foot, following his own search pattern, constantly calling Hunter's name.

I'm not really sure how much time had passed since I had talked to Linda the first time, but it seemed like just a few minutes when I saw her driving back down the road toward us. She stopped and told us Buster came home but Hunter wasn't with him and - most importantly - Buster was soaking wet!

The information was passed on by radio to the search teams and they immediately headed back to search the creek again, as it had already been searched once. From what I was told, two of the officers finally spotted Hunter floating face down in a small pool of water only about three or four feet deep - the rest of the creek was totally dry! They both jumped in after him, shorting out their radios. Somehow, they managed to call for assistance and soon, the ambulance arrived at their location. The EMT's immediately began efforts to revive him and the race to the hospital was on.

During this time, I was standing next to a police officer when the call came in over his radio that they had found Hunter! My heart was still pounding but a wave of relief washed over me and I wanted to find Eldon and tell him. I didn't know that Eldon and Chris had met there at the creek just about the same time the officers found Hunter and they were there, standing beside the ambulance as they pulled him from the water. Through radio communications, we were told that they were taking Hunter to the hospital in Springdale.

Everyone piled into different cars and hurried to the hospital. This might sound crazy but, for the life of me, I still can't tell you to this day how I got there. That space of time is a huge blur for me. I DO remember praying, though. It wasn't a fancy prayer by any means; just the same thing over and over and over again, "God, please let him be ok. Please let him be ok. Please let him be ok." My mother shared with me later that she was praying the same prayer.

We all arrived about the same time the ambulance pulled up to the ER entrance and I do remember standing outside, watching them take the gurney from the vehicle. He was lying so still on that big bed with an oxygen mask over his face. I called out, "Hunter, Grammy loves you!" as they wheeled him inside.

We walked into the ER waiting area and a nurse quickly escorted us to a small private room off to one side, away from the larger waiting area and prying eyes. It was a tiny room with several chairs and a small table in one corner. There was a box of tissues on the table. I remember sitting down and watching the door as other family members began to arrive. The nurse would bring them back to the little room and we would hug and cry and pray. My sister, Karen, and her husband, Dan, soon appeared in the doorway. There was more hugging and crying. I hated that little room.

I remember looking at a clock out in the hallway once but I really had no sense of how long we'd been there. Time had no meaning for me that night. It was a terrible waiting game of the worst kind for all of us and I kept thinking things like, "I hope he doesn't get pneumonia. I hope he doesn't have any broken bones. I could just paddle his little bottom for running off and scaring us all half to death like that!"

We were on pins and needles as a nurse would come in every few minutes and tell us they were still "working on him". Word had quickly spread throughout the community and the emergency room was bursting with other relatives, precious friends and church family.

Chris led a group of young men, and Greta led a group of girls from our church called cell groups. They were mentoring the group members from junior high until they graduate high school. Both cell groups came to the hospital that night, along with many other young people that had come with them to offer their support. Together, those young people formed circles outside in the parking lot, unashamedly holding hands and praying for Hunter.

My dear friend, Kathy, heard the news somehow and found me in that little room. Our kids had grown up together and I was comforted to see her. We stood in the hall outside the little waiting room, talking and hugging.

When the doctor finally did appear through the big double doors and came toward us, I could tell by the look on his face that it was bad. I knew it. He offered his condolences and told us they were never able to resuscitate him. Hunter was dead.

I was standing outside the little room in the hallway and at that very moment, even though there were many people around me, I could not hear or utter a sound. I felt as if I was in a vacuum. I couldn't catch my breath and my knees gave way as I slowly slid down the wall and landed in a sobbing heap on the floor. I remember looking up into Kathy's eyes. She grabbed me and held me tight as we cried. The silent vacuum gradually gave way to muffled sound and I heard people crying all around me. All at once, from the crowd of people, I heard my mother gasp and cry out, "Oh God! No!"

Eldon was still inside the little room with Chris and Greta and his voice echoed out through the hallway in sobs, "Son, we can NOT let this create a root of bitterness in our hearts. We will stand firm in God's love as a family and we WILL get through this terrible thing!"

That was my pain and it felt like an awful pit I could not claw myself out of. It was the first realization for me that I would never see Hunter here on this earth again. That precious little boy, so full of life, was gone from us.

As word of Hunter's death spread to the others outside the little room, I heard wave after wave of gasps, moans and soft crying. Shock and disbelief washed over my family as we realized there was nothing else to be done. It was over.

How could such a thing have happened? How could this day have begun so great and ended with the death of our precious grandson? It was too much for me to comprehend. I looked into the faces of my family to try to find some answers but those faces were also wet with tears and twisted with their own pain. It was the pain of separation.

A short time later, someone came through the door and asked us if we'd like to see Hunter. We all followed Chris and Greta as a family back to the exam room where they had worked for so long trying to revive him. His little body lay on the bed so still. He looked like he was just sleeping. He had no marks on his body, no bruising, nothing. His beautiful brown hair was still slightly wet. We all circled that gurney and touched and caressed his little hands, his little feet, and his face. We all cried. Actually, it was more like wailing. Even though I didn't realize it at the time, we were saying goodbye, each in our own way.

Finally, we left the hospital, car after car in a solemn, silent caravan back to our house.

We didn't know what else to do. Chris and Greta wanted to initially go to their house to shower. Understandably, they needed to be alone with each other. Everyone else went home, but my kids came to our house and stayed the night. We sat together in the den for such a long time, just crying and holding each other. It was a terrible thing we had just experienced but we took some sort of comfort in just being in the same room. We were together as a family but we were all in terrible pain.

chapter two
The Grief

It was very late that evening when we all finally tried to sleep, but I'm fairly certain no one did. I kept playing the events, sights and sounds over and over in my mind; the ambulance siren wailing as it drove away to the hospital, the looks on the policemen's faces, and even the people at the hospital. That might sound strange, but I think I was just trying to keep my brain busy or find some sort of comfort. There was none for either Eldon or me. We could not sleep. We just held each other as the clock ticked – hour after hour. We were unable to talk about what had happened. We just cried, slowly watching that terrible night turn into the next day.

When morning came, Chris and Greta walked up to our house and we all began the business of getting through that awful day. There were arrangements to be made, people to call and so forth. All of us just moved like zombies around the house, not even knowing where to begin. It was difficult to think clearly.

During the next couple of days, someone was there with us, expressing their condolences or asking what they could do for us. Some didn't ask; they just did. They answered the telephone and answered the door, kept track of who called or visited, and set the food out so we could eat. I barely functioned at all. I don't remember any anger or frustration at that point; I was numb but I could cry. There were always tears.

Those first few days are always an especially difficult time for those of us left behind. We wrestle with our own emotions and thoughts as we see and talk to family members or friends that are doing much the same thing. Then, there are the folks that are sad for you but aren't directly involved or can't bear to be. Most people want to be sensitive to your grief BUT there are bills that still have to be paid, food that has to be prepared, and so on and so forth. Life goes on. I hated that. For me, life didn't go on; it stood absolutely and totally still. For me, life had changed forever and I couldn't understand why everyone else didn't know or acknowledge that. I wanted everyone else to be sad; not just our family. I wanted the whole world to stop and mourn Hunter's death with us.

If you ever do any research at all about grief, the one thing you'll quickly find out is that everyone has a theory about it. Some of those theories are diametrically opposed to others and there are many. Many have done intensive studies on the subject and there are books, audio recordings and Internet articles galore.

The most well-known seems to be the widely accepted "five stages of grief" discussed in the book "On Death and Dying" by Elizabeth Kubler-Ross.[1]

The stages are listed as: denial and isolation, anger, bargaining, depression and acceptance. Of the hundreds I found online, one grief website listed the stages as: shock or disbelief, denial, bargaining, guilt, anger, depression, and acceptance and hope. Later, I will share more about these stages.

I am not a trained psychiatrist or counselor, but I have lived through the pain and grief and I'm here to tell you that my "stages" didn't follow any exact guidelines or order. Yours may not either. In fact, I vividly remember when, many months after Hunter's death, someone asked me how Chris and Greta were doing and what "stage of grief" I thought they were in. That person meant well I'm sure, but I'm also quite sure I didn't hide the look of utter amazement on my face! I had no clue about what stage I was in, let alone Chris and Greta! I think well-meaning people get too caught up in the "stage" thing, and, sometimes, people simply aren't very good "comforters" to begin with.

Actually, it's a fact that you may vary widely in your emotions from one day to the next, or one minute to the next. You could be feeling angry and depressed and then something might make you remember something precious about your loved one and you would feel happy and uplifted for a while. It is a roller coaster ride, to say the least; up and down and sometimes even sideways.

My caution here: Don't focus on those stages and don't worry about trying to figure all that out when you are still in so much pain. The important thing is that you realize these emotions are very normal and you should try to work through them as you are able.

That reminds me of the little story "Footprints in the Sand".[2] I'm sure you've heard of it. It has become very popular and you can find it everywhere these days on coffee cups, plaques, bookmarks, cards and stationery. It is the story of someone's dream as they looked back on their life, seeing two sets of footprints where the Lord walked with them through the sands of their life. During the hardest and most terrible times in his life, the person notices only one set of footprints in the sand. He questions the Lord, asking why He would leave him at the times he needed Him the most. The Lord tells him that it was through those most difficult times that "I carried you". How true that was for me! Sometimes it was all I could do just to take the next breath. Although I wasn't consciously aware of it then (much like the person in the poem) I can clearly see now that the Lord was carrying me through those days. My feet weren't even touching the ground. I was being quietly carried along by the God of the Universe, my Creator, the One who knew my pain better than anyone.

During the days leading up to the funeral, the doorbell and the phone rang constantly and I found myself just standing in the middle of the living room floor in zombie mode; not knowing what to do first or where to go next. That is the mind-numbing pain of grief and sorrow. Mostly, those days were just filled with tears. I thought I would never stop crying.

We went to the funeral home. Greta and Chris had decided to dress Hunter in his "jammies" and he really looked like he was just lying there, taking a nap. Greta put the fuzzy stuffed kitty he slept with under his little arm. It was hard for me to look at, but then, somehow, seeing him like that helped comfort me. I knew Hunter was already in the presence of the King of Kings and Lord of Lords; I was just looking at his "earth suit" (as Chris would describe it) and it brought me peace and comfort. I can't explain why, it just did. That's another thing I've realized - what comforts you doesn't necessarily comfort others and, it's important that you give yourself some grace and allow yourself to feel or be comforted in those times.

There were flowers to be ordered. Chris and Greta talked about the service with our pastors. There was music to pick out and pictures to select for a memorial video. Then, there was the actual funeral service ahead and the cemetery plot to purchase and all those people to deal with. And again, all those tears. It seemed like I would just gain my composure, only to lose it again. With everything that had to be done and all the places we had to go, I still could not focus for any length of time. My mind would constantly wander and many times I thought I was going crazy but I wasn't; it was that pain. It was unlike anything I had ever experienced before or since then and it was excruciating. I couldn't pray; I cried. I tried to manage a smile but tears came instead. I couldn't sleep; I cried.

It was during one of those days that I finally picked up my Bible and turned quite unintentionally to the eleventh chapter of John and began reading about Lazarus. If you're not familiar with the story, allow me to give you the 'paraphrased by Pam' version.

It was a well-known fact that Lazarus and his two sisters, Mary and Martha, were very good friends of Jesus and he had stayed at their house in Bethany on many occasions when he passed through the area.

Lazarus grew very ill and, in fact, he died. The grieving sisters (feeling that pain of separation, I'm sure) sent word to Jerusalem for Jesus to come but He stayed away for two more days before He made plans to return to Bethany, which was less than two miles away. Jesus told the disciples that Lazarus had "fallen asleep" and He was going back to "wake him up". The disciples thought Jesus was talking about natural sleep at first, but later He made it clear to them that Lazarus had actually died. When Jesus and His disciples finally made it back to Bethany, Lazarus had been in the tomb for four days.

After hearing that Jesus was headed back their way, Martha went out to meet him. She gave Jesus a lot of trouble about not coming back when they first sent word. (Remember though, she was hurting.) She knew that He could have come back sooner, healed Lazarus from his sickness and he wouldn't have died. Jesus told her that her brother would rise again and she acknowledged that, saying, "Yes, I know he will, Lord, in the resurrection." Martha was referring to the promise of the last days when the Bible tells us in I Thessalonians 4:16 that the "dead in Christ will rise up to meet Him in the air". Back in John 11, verse 25, you can read how Jesus tried to make her understand what He meant but in the end, He just had to SHOW her. He had to show them all.

Martha told Mary that Jesus had finally arrived and she went out to meet Him with all the mourners following behind her. (At least, back then, people weren't afraid to cry with you!) She fell at His feet and the Bible tells us she cried. She had lost her beloved brother and she was grieving. Jesus asked her where Lazarus was and He was shown the tomb. It is recorded that "Jesus wept". That word "wept" in the Greek denotes quiet weeping, like tears that slowly run down your cheeks – not wailing or loud sobbing.

A small aside here: It has been discovered and documented that the composition of tears of sorrow are chemically different from tears of joy. You don't think God knows the difference between the two? You'd better believe He does! He understands them better than we understand them ourselves.

Back to Jesus at the tomb - Everyone thought He was crying because Lazarus was dead and verse 36 even tells us that the Jews said, "See how he loved him!" Personally, I think Jesus wept tears of sorrow because He didn't want to bring Lazarus back from Paradise. Let me stop here and explain why I believe that.

In our humanity we, just like Mary and Martha, cling to life with great tenacity and most usually, it is very difficult for us to see anything beyond that death or separation, especially at first. Jesus (God in the flesh) saw the bigger picture because He's omniscient – He knows the past, the present and the future. Jesus knew that Lazarus was already in Paradise (2 Corinthians 5:8) and I think for Him to bring him back, knowing he would have to experience death a second time, caused Him to weep. That's just my personal take on why he actually cried.

Nevertheless, they rolled back the stone from the tomb and Jesus called Lazarus to come out and he did. He came out alive with all his grave clothes still on and the neighbors celebrated and rejoiced along with the family.

As I read the story of Lazarus that day, it lifted me up and I was encouraged somehow. (See? Another little encouragement!) I wouldn't have been able to explain why then but looking back on it now, I understand it better. By reading that account in the Bible and opening my heart and mind, it comforted me to realize that Jesus had experienced the same emotion of grief, if not for different reasons. I had received comfort by the Holy Spirit (THE Comforter) and God's Word which, the scriptures tell us "never returns void".

That story just confirmed what I already knew; that Hunter was already in Paradise with the Lord and I did recall the verse in 2 Corinthians, chapter 5 about being "absent from the body is to be present with the Lord". Although I missed him terribly and my heart still ached so much because he was gone from us, why would I want to take him away from that and bring him back, only to face death again at a later time?

chapter three
Trust in the "Yord"

I grew up in the church; my husband is an ordained minister of the Gospel. Jesus Christ is my Lord and Savior and I believe in a literal Heaven and hell but nothing in my entire Christian life had quite prepared me for what I felt after Hunter died.

In one of the many times I played that Sunday over and over again in my mind, I remembered that it had also been the day that Hunter had memorized his first Bible verse. I'll try to explain why this was such a momentous event. Hunter was always a very busy boy and he didn't have time for memorizing Bible verses. He wanted to play or draw or run, jump and climb trees or just be outside doing something. Each Sunday before that day, it was always the same thing; he was asked about the new Bible verse on the Share Card the teacher had sent home with him but he just couldn't remember it. In fact, he had never memorized a single verse.

That Sunday was different though. That particular day, he ran into our house after church, yelling at the top of his little lungs because he was so excited (Hunter had a problem pronouncing his L's). He stood up in front of us and proclaimed with all his might, "Trust in da Yord wiff all your heart!" as he pointed to his little chest.

We were all so proud he had finally memorized a verse that Greta let him call everyone that afternoon so he could recite it for them over the phone. We all shared in his joyful accomplishment and, remembering the look on his little face as he said it over and over, there was no doubt he was exceptionally proud of himself.

I look back on that scene now and see the hand of God so clearly. Even before the funeral, Chris, Eldon and I had all been discussing the "it is appointed for a man once to die" scripture and God's plans for all our lives. The more and more we talked, the more it seemed to me that the very verse Hunter was so proud to quote for all of us that day might just have been learned and recited purely to prepare us for what lay ahead for us. Let me remind you of the whole verse…"Trust in the Lord with all your heart and *lean not on your own understanding* (emphasis mine). In all your ways acknowledge Him, and He will make your paths straight." Proverbs 3:5-6.

I began to recite that over and over in my mind and truly dwell on each word. Those two verses brought me great comfort then and still do today. I have come to realize that if I believe that God has a plan for my life then I have to believe He also had a plan for Hunter's life, as short as it was. I could not trust in my own understanding to make sense of Hunter's death because it didn't make sense to me. But, if I could just trust God with 'all my heart' and not try to figure it out on my own, He promised me that, even though I might not understand it all, He would direct me nonetheless.

If you too are on that grief journey right now, have you been trying to make sense of it all? Feels like your head might explode, doesn't it? Trust me, I know that feeling. It's not that we can't ask those questions, especially the "WHY?" ones. In our humanity, we have to ask. It just means that we may never get the answers this side of Heaven and that is something we have to accept and deal with as flesh and blood human beings. There were many other promises that God's Word blessed me with in the weeks, even months following his death but none stuck with me like Proverbs 3:5-6. To this day, my family still calls that "Hunter's verse".

Another thing that really stayed with me was the fact that our church family was truly so supportive and loving through this awful time in our lives. The care and love we experienced was the most amazing thing! The church we attend in Northwest Arkansas is very large with many members and because it is so big, it is not unusual at all for people to attend there and to never have met each other. I had heard many sermons at Fellowship about the importance of representing Jesus to those in need and being the "hands and feet" of Christ. The wonderful thing is that the principle is not only taught there but it is lived out in the lives of the members. Our church has a wonderful support system set up for people in need but that was the first time I experienced it for myself and I thank God everyday for people that dedicate their lives in true service to others and live it out daily. We always need love and support but especially during the journey of grief.

I mentioned earlier about those that came to our home and literally ran it for days on end so we could focus on other things. They kept lists of who brought food, flowers or gifts so we could thank people later and even answered the phone and took messages. They took such good care of us. One good friend came to our place of business and sat there for days answering the phone, gently explaining to customers why we were closed indefinitely. I didn't realize it at the time but now I can look back and see how people tried to care for us. (We just don't seem to take very good care of ourselves when we're hurting.) Some made sure we were eating properly – we wouldn't have otherwise, I'm sure. Others re-minded us of God's love through scripture. I would go into the kitchen and open a cabinet door to find little sticky notes inside, some with a scripture verse on it, others with just words of encouragement and love. They were everywhere in the house – on the mirrors in the bathrooms, inside closet doors, everywhere! It was amazing. There were wonderful poems and letters left lying on tables and sent to us by mail and I know many prayers were lifted to God's throne on our behalf. I could fill a complete chapter just telling you of the wonderful and caring things that people did for our family; the funeral home, the monument company, the florist and countless others. Whether big or small, they all exhibited wonderful expressions of love and support.

This was not only humbling to me but truly amazing that people would do such unselfish things, and some didn't even know us personally. We all experienced a true out-pouring of Christ's love; people being the hands and feet of Christ to us. It was not only a wonderful testimony of our friends and church family but of God's loving guidance and support, comforting us through the kindness of others. Can you see where our needs were met and our "paths directed"? I certainly can now.

The day of Hunter's funeral was beautiful and full of September sunshine. When we pulled up to the church, it looked like we were having a regular Sunday morning service. The parking lot was filled with cars. Everyone was already seated in the sanctuary when we came in and we were directed to our seats up front. We all sat down and the service began.

The audio/visual department at our church had put together a little video montage of Hunter accompanied by the song "I Can Only Imagine" by the group Mercy Me. It was very moving and as I watched, I could recall where every single picture was taken and when. Seeing his little face was so precious to me but as I listened to the words of the song, I began to think about Hunter already being in the presence of the Lord God Almighty. I wondered what he might be doing at that moment and immediately thought of him running as hard and fast as he could, smiling and laughing, free from all care or worry. I almost smiled.

Our pastors conducted the service with amazing tenderness and compassion. With smiles on their faces, they reminded us of the day to come when we would see Hunter again, and I went back for just a minute to Mary and Martha and poor old Lazarus. His sisters wanted him back so desperately and they probably *still* ended up having to sit through *two* funerals!

As the days passed, I found myself able to sleep a little and I was even praying again, talking to the Lord and asking Him to help me with the pain. I asked Him to comfort my family in their pain and I even remember one night I asked Him to "kiss Hunter" for me. I still missed him terribly and the pain of my grief was still very real, and honestly, at times, overwhelming. I couldn't imagine I would ever feel better.

chapter four
Grief Shared

As the days wore on, we still pretty much stayed together at the house, except to sleep. We had closed our business temporarily and none of the kids went to their jobs. It warms my heart and blesses me to think that my children would find comfort in staying with each other at our home. I know the pain was terrible for them too but, somehow, we took comfort in being together. As a mother, I always liked to think that my kids were close but this was different. During that time, I believe my kids united in a way few brothers and sisters ever do. I can truly say our whole family bonded in an extraordinary way. There were still some painful things to do like selecting a headstone and arranging for the burial plot. We all supported and helped each other do what had to be done.

I'm not sure how it all came about or whose idea it was, but there was a certain lady that does videography. Somehow she was contacted about making a video of Hunter's life. We began pooling our pictures to provide her with material to work with. The end result was an amazing half-hour movie, some still pictures and some videos of my precious grandson and the short time he spent here on this earth with us; birthday parties and

Christmases past, family dinners and even bath times. Each picture or video set to the perfect song was truly a blessing to watch but, as you might imagine, I cried uncontrollably the first time I saw it. We all did. To this day, I have not met the wonderful woman that composed that video and blessed us so much with it. What a gift!

Let me encourage you here to try and memorialize your precious loved one in some meaningful way. Sometimes, especially at first, the memories might not be very sweet but, as time passes and you begin to heal, they will become a wonderful reminder of better times and you can return to them repeatedly. There's no rush and you certainly don't have to make a video like we did. Perhaps journaling your feelings in a notebook or writing a letter to your loved one would appeal to you more. A scrapbook is another wonderful way to preserve those precious memories with pictures and little keepsakes. You could also just keep a box filled with the things you want to return to from time to time to look at and remember, including the cards and letters you received but haven't had the time or the inclination to go through. One precious lady told me that she was so "out of it" during the funeral, she didn't remember anything. Having a video her church made to go back to later and watch helped her fill in the "gap". A daughter that lost her father took all of his ties and sewed them together to make a coverlet. The possibilities are endless. Something along these lines will most certainly help you deal and heal.

As more time passed, things began to settle down a bit and we returned to our jobs and everyday life. My family and I began to discuss the possibility of going to some sort of counseling together. We met as a family with a trained counselor on staff at our church a month or so after Hunter's death. He was wonderful to us and we were all glad we went. It was difficult for us to talk at first but we felt safe there. We talked about a few things but I remember we all still cried a lot.

Counseling is a very good idea and I would encourage you in this if you haven't already gone. I don't care how long it's been since you lost your loved one. Counseling or some sort of grief support group will likely help you more than you would ever think possible.

Let me just remind you again; everyone deals with their grief and pain differently. Even being the close-knit family that we were, everyone was feeling something different - some of us were in very different places. You must try your best to be sensitive to that, as this will greatly minimize conflicts that could arise. I wrote earlier that everyone's grief is unique – just like fingerprints. You should NOT measure your grief or recovery by someone else's nor should you expect them to feel exactly as you are feeling. That's not a burden you need to weigh yourself down with and counseling really helped me realize that.

It was suggested that we should, at some point, enter a support group setting where we could meet and interact with others that had lost loved ones. There was just such a group meeting on

Monday nights at our church called GriefShare[3] and our counselor encouraged us to come and see what we thought about attending the whole series. The group met early (5:30 p.m.) because they served a meal before we started, and then there was a short video and discussion. They sometimes broke up into smaller groups for more specific discussions. I asked my husband and the kids what they thought about going. Everyone was in agreement so we signed up.

We began the very first session in January, four months after Hunter's death. We all entered the room slowly, almost shy, not really knowing what to expect. There were a few people already there, filling their plates with food and talking. The leaders greeted us and introduced themselves, then directed us to the food and helped us find seats. None of us was eating very healthy at home those days but they always made sure we got a good meal at GriefShare.

The meeting finally began and it was clear to me that we had made the right decision. I remember learning some very important things that night:

We were in a safe place and everything was to be held in strict confidence. We didn't have to worry about anything we said going outside of that room.

It was OK to cry (hence the MANY boxes of tissues sitting around). Tears were actually encouraged and not to be apologized for.

Our individuality was stressed over and over – the fact that every one handles their grief differently is very important to remember.

As we shared our stories, we were also reminded not to take anyone else's grief home with us.

We began with introductions and shared a brief summary of our story; who our loved one was and how they died. We shared pictures, watched a short video and then broke up into a smaller group where we could talk and share more at length. There was a couple that had lost a newborn, wives missing husbands and vice versa. There were grown children that had lost a parent and all these people were hurting too. There were even a few that were in so much pain they couldn't bring themselves to speak at all. They just sat and cried. Such overwhelming, undeniable pain!

Even though I knew that my family and I weren't the only ones hurting, it was still tough to hear the different stories. That was a hard night and I had to keep cautioning myself about getting wrapped up in anyone else's story or pain. Some might say, "Why would I want to go and listen to all that pain when I've got plenty of my own?!?" All I can tell you is that, hearing what others faced or are facing, gives you an insight you've never had before into your own grief. Not only that but, when you share your story with someone else and vice versa, you realize there is a certain connection or bond formed – especially in a support group setting. It's really not so much the "misery loves company" attitude, but more like "we're all in this together".

That night before we left, one of the leaders shared a saying with the group that I have never forgotten. She said, "Remember, grief shared is grief diminished." That was exactly what we were doing there – *sharing* our grief and pain and getting it out into the open. You'll find, if you haven't already, that after the funeral and a few weeks pass, everyone else goes on about their business while you're still working through the terrible void the death of your loved one has created. They don't particularly want to talk about it with you, especially if you might cry. That makes most people uncomfortable and they would rather avoid that unpleasantness. They just want you to get back to "normal". They don't realize that things won't ever be normal again.

No one there had a magic pill we could take to make it all go away and they weren't going to "fix" everything for us but they were going to walk alongside us for a short time. Somehow, I felt better. Not because these people had lost someone and were hurting too but because they were there *with me*. They listened to me and I listened to them. As we shared pictures of our loved ones and commented on each, we came together and formed a relationship of sharing and listening and, each night following, we continued to share and the grief continued to diminish.

Because it is easy to let your grief isolate you (especially if you're angry), it's easy to get stuck there and never move on if you're not careful. My dear friend Carie is no stranger to grief and loss, having experienced the death of her infant son,

Andrew, and dreadful divorce years later. She reminded me once that, "Satan is our enemy and he loves the lonely and independent." Truer words were never spoken! Take extra care not to shut yourself off or isolate yourself in your grief or you run the risk of making that your identity. Your grief is NOT your identity so if you are feeling "stuck" or you just can't move forward, I would encourage you to begin monitoring your thinking *and* your behavior. This is another reason you should journal, at least for a while. You have a choice, you can be (as someone once said) "bitter or you can be better" and you'll have a hard time ever getting better if you stay in a pit where your only identity is your grief.

GriefShare was support at its finest ("dealing and healing" I call it). Attending that group helped me realize that whether the death is expected or not, it is still just as painful. Whether the person that died was young or old, it was still painful to those left behind. Although I didn't realize it, I was already beginning my journey towards healing just by attending that group, sharing and talking things out. I was actually beginning to take a few baby steps forward.

chapter five
The Journey

I think that first night of GriefShare was also the first time I realized that my personal journey through this grief was going to be directly related to my relationship with Jesus Christ. I remember Chris asking me later, "Mom, I really don't know how people make it through something like this without the Lord." "How do they?" I told him, "Many of them don't, son. Many of them don't."

If you research some statistics, you might find reports of a higher divorce rate among couples that lose a child. Some people turn to drugs or alcohol to dull the pain and hope that will enable them to somehow cope with the loss of a loved one. Some people just "drop out" of life entirely (there's that isolation!) and some even take their own lives. Then there are the ones that experience the pain and realize they can't come through it on their own. They know that they need a supernatural strength, a higher power; someone to "carry" them through it.

There is no one that knows the grief of loss like the Maker of the universe. After all, He sent his only Son to die for us. Remember the "Footprints" poem? He *can* and *will* carry us through. You will notice I said *through.* "Stuffing" the grief and refusing to address it will only delay the whole process and, when it resurfaces sometime later, it can have disastrous results. It's important to realize that you must go through the grief. It cannot be avoided.

Let's go back a moment and run through those stages again but, instead of stages, let's think of them as a journey of different emotions.

SHOCK OR DISBELIEF/DENIAL ~

Shock is certainly an emotion that I think most everyone experiences in the death of a loved one, especially when it is as unexpected as a car crash, a drowning, a heart attack or something of the sort. We've all experienced that shock of the unexpected. Denial is refusing to believe or accept a fact.[4] The reality of my pain was that Hunter was gone and I wouldn't see him again on this earth. I can see why some people would want to deny a loved one's death if they thought they might never see them again!

Death makes us face our own mortality and realize that we aren't really in control, even though we'd like to think that we are. Death is an absolute fact and we are powerless to change that. I have a little acrostic that summarizes denial perfectly. It goes like this:

D   Disables our feelings and freezes our emotions.

E   Energy lost (excessive worrying or being fearful can waste precious energy).

N   Negates growth (we can become "stuck" and find moving forward difficult).

I   Isolates us as we reject truth (attending a support group helps you confront your true feelings).

A   Alienates us from relationships (satan is the father and master of lies and will try to convince you that others can't help you and you should handle this alone).

L   Lengthens the pain and allows it to fester. This hinders healing.

Disbelief or denial can sometime cause you to look up when the door opens, as you expect your loved one to come walking in.

Just remember this…you can't heal a wound by pretending it's not there.

ANGER ~

Now if you're at all familiar with the story of Job – can you honestly tell me there was anyone with a better reason to be angry?

Right at the outset, in chapter one, the Sabeans came and stole all Job's donkeys and oxen and they slaughtered the servants tending them. Word came that fire had fallen from the sky and burned up every one of his sheep and the servants tending them as well. Another guy comes to tell him that the Chaldeans swung by and stole every camel Job had and killed all those servants. Then, just when

I would imagine Job was thinking to himself, "What else could possibly go wrong today?" along comes another person to tell him that all of his children had been gathered in his eldest son's house for a celebration when a mighty wind blew the house down around them all and they were all dead. Notice in verse twenty – "Job tore his robe and shaved his head." That's pain, folks; real, grieving pain. But what does Job do? The Bible tells us that he fell to the ground in *worship* (verse 22). "In all this, Job did not sin by charging God with wrongdoing."

Let's be honest here, shall we? If that had been me, I believe I would've been angry, and not just a little angry either! Now, looking back at the time right after Hunter's death, I realize there was a brief period when I must admit I was mad at God. I think it was anger mixed with the pain of the loss. Anger is an appropriate emotion in the journey of grief and it's alright to be angry for a while. The most important thing here is to be honest enough to admit it and then deal with that anger. God is certainly big enough to handle it and He does understand, I promise you.

I remember one day, many months later, I was having a conversation with a customer and he asked me if I ever got mad at God for "taking" Hunter. I'm sure he wanted me to give him an explanation for why it had happened. I had to tell him what I had realized earlier and that I still believe to this day; the Bible tells us in John 10:10 that we have an enemy that "comes only to steal and kill and destroy". God didn't *take* Hunter. It was the enemy of our souls who seeks to devour us like a roaring lion and he did it all alone. Did God *allow* it? Yes, I believe so – for reasons only HE knows. Don't get me wrong – asking the why questions are certainly appropriate and you can ask; you may not get an answer and, even if you did, would it be the one that would make everything all better again? In God's perfect plan, His infinite, omniscient will, He allows things for our growth and benefit. Just like He *allowed* Job to experience what he did. But you can't stop there.

In chapter 13, verse 15, Job said, "Though He (God) slay me, yet will I trust Him." I began to find story after story in God's Word about those who had gone through horrendous things, but still trusted God with the outcome and allowed Him to work His perfect plan for their lives. And you know, in every single story, that person came out stronger, wiser and most usually, in much closer relationship with God.

I remembered that in the Bible, David lost a child too. Not his grandson, it was his *son*. In Psalms 31:15 he boldly and wisely tells God "My times are in Your hand." Sounds like someone that realized he wasn't the master of his own destiny to me. (Do you need to go back and read the "DENIAL" part again?) I found true comfort in that and I began to read those verses in Psalms aloud and pray them back to God.

Reading the Psalms when you don't feel like praying on your own can be very helpful. Many times, the Psalms can say it for you when you don't have the words yourself. I prayed the Psalms a LOT.

BARGAINING~

I can tell you truthfully here that I never found myself bargaining with God about Hunter's death. By the time I realized Hunter was gone, it was too late to do any bargaining anyway. That's not to say that, if I'd thought of it in time, I wouldn't have. I'm fairly certain I would have tried to make some sort of deal with God for Hunter's life if I'd had the opportunity. The bargaining approach is all based around works. You know, "If you'll do this, then I'll do that." That won't work. Better to sincerely cry out to God and ask Him for His help in the situation.

Someone asked me if I had ever tried to "bargain away" my pain or the pain of my children. I did pray and earnestly did plead for an *end* to it but never tried to bargain it completely away from any of us. That is the human side of us; wanting it to go away or be over. Again, that is where GriefShare helped me realize early on that this was something that had to be gone through and there is no quick fix to grief. To postpone it only means it will take longer for you to heal properly.

The Scripture verse that seems most appropriate for this emotion was Isaiah 55:8-9. "My (God's) thoughts are not your thoughts, neither are your ways My ways." Well, I can agree with that. For all the things we DON'T understand in this life, God understands PERFECTLY. If you read the whole chapter, I promise a light will begin to dawn regarding God's sovereignty and omnipotence. Just know that it is very human to want to make some sort of deal, but covenant and bargaining are two completely different things. There are plenty of stories in the Bible of someone trying to make a deal with the God of the universe, only to have it backfire horribly. Read about Jephthah and how his bargain with God turned out in Judges 11.

GUILT~

Oh yeah, did I struggle with that! I called it the 'what ifs' but it was guilt just the same. "What if" I'd taken Hunter inside the house with me that day "What if" I'd told Eldon to go get Hunter outside and bring him in? "What if" I'd just been more careful, more watchful? After all, they were at my house. What if, what if, what if? The list went on and on and I will tell you, I struggled with that for a very long time.

You may feel condemned by your guilt but Romans 8:33-35 tells you otherwise. Just listen to this passage from The Message: "And who would dare tangle with God by messing with one of God's chosen? Who would dare even to point a finger? The One who died for us – who was raised to life for us – is in the presence of God at this very moment sticking up for us. Do you think anyone is going to be able to drive a wedge between us and Christ's love for us? There is no way! Not trouble, not hard times, not hatred, not hunger, not homelessness, not bullying threats, not backstabbing." Then comes verse 37 (I LOVE it)! "None of this fazes us because *Jesus loves us* (emphasis mine)."

If you are having feelings of guilt, you must decide if they are true or false. False guilt (like my 'what ifs') comes from the enemy of our soul. Recognize that condemnation can drive you to despair and away from God. If you have some real guilt about something that happened, something you said, or whatever it might be, work through it. Conviction can draw you closer to God. A word of warning here: It's very natural to have those feelings of guilt and 'what ifs' but it's important for you to know that, if you own that guilt too long, it can allow the enemy a substantial victory and even lead you into depression. In a GriefShare video entitled, "The Uniqueness of Grief, Part 1", Dr. Jack Hayford tells us, "True guilt, if dealt with properly, will actually lead us to God's forgiveness and right standing with Him." Realize that you did the best you could, with what you had or knew at the time and receive the forgiveness that is yours in Christ.

Actually, it was my son Chris that opened my eyes to this one. After much thought about it (and some 'what ifs' of his own, I'm sure) he shared this amazing truth with me and I believe he summed it up beautifully for us all. Chris said, "Mom, I really believe now with all my heart that

September 26th was Hunter's appointed day to die. I think that even if we had somehow known that was the day and I sat, holding him all day to prevent it, it still would've happened some way." He had finally worked through his 'what ifs'. That was a pretty amazing statement that Chris made. For some of you, what he said may sound a little questionable, but I sincerely believe that God is the Blessed Controller of *all* things. Just read about God's perfect knowledge of man in Psalm 139.

There may have been unfinished business, words you wished had said or things you've thought of since that you wanted that person to know. After all, an unexpected death sometimes leaves the ones left behind wishing they'd told their loved one they loved them more often, taken that trip they'd always wanted to take or done this or that and so on. Please don't carry that false guilt around with you for too long. Begin to write those things down in that journal you started or perhaps write a letter to your loved one as I mentioned earlier. My dear friend, Jennie would tell you, "Get it all out and write it all down!" Write with the confidence that no one else will ever read it. Did you want to ask for forgiveness? Ask for it in your letter/journal. Did you want to express your love or anger about something? Express it in your journal/letter and let those feelings (and possibly) tears surface. That is really important and, although you might not think so, once you begin writing, you'll be amazed at what can and does come out.

Writing can be extremely therapeutic and the wonderful part about it is that, after you write or journal your feelings, whether it's everyday, every week, or whatever, you can return to those pages occasionally and see how you are progressing.

It will become apparent to you that slowly, day by day, you are putting one foot in front of the other and your journey to healing is underway. In fact, a journal was the first gift I received after the funeral. My friend, Kathy, gave me a prayer journal to begin jotting down my feelings and prayers. I'm still using it and I go back to the beginning ever so often even now just to see how far I've traveled on my journey and how faithful God has been (and continues to be) to me.

There you have it. Sounds almost too simple, and sometimes easier said than done, to apply to your situation but I promise you, it does apply. So recognize that guilt, that condemnation, those 'what ifs', and deal with them. Then let them go and you will slowly but surely (and thankfully) realize that God is in control.

DEPRESSION~

At this point, I must refer you to the book of Lamentations 3:22-23. "Because of the Lord's great love we are not consumed, for His compassions never fail. They are new every morning, great is Your faithfulness." This is another one of my all-time favorites. Was I hanging on to that? You bet! In fact, one of the songs we all sang together at

Hunter's funeral was "Great is Thy Faithfulness,"[5] a wonderful old hymn and very special to me, especially in light of those verses in Lamentations.

Some anxiety and depression are unavoidable, I think. In an earlier chapter, you'll remember that I described myself as "numb"; walking around, forgetting why I entered a room or spacing out. I've heard people describe it in many ways and with many different terms – sick, a darkness or heaviness, zombie-like, oppressed, and unfeeling. I had one man tell me that, after his wife died, he found himself stopping at green lights and running red ones. When he shared this with our grief group, several people nodded their heads and said, "Thank goodness! I thought I was the only one that did that!" The list is long and I'm sure you could add your own things to it. You're not going crazy; grief does strange things to a person.

It has been suggested that death and grief was not part of God's original plan and I don't have trouble believing that at all. Death and its pain began after the fall in the Garden. No wonder it hurts so much. We are only flesh and blood, so when you feel like the pain might not ever go away or it seems like there is nothing to hang on to or for, remember that God IS faithful and the healing WILL come. It just takes time. For some, it takes longer than others but time will be your friend one day. My pastor said it this way: **"YOU MAY GRIEVE HARD BUT HOPE BIG!"** Seven little words that sum it up much better than I ever could. How profound.

I remember one day Eldon and I had gone to spend some quiet time at the lake. The parking lot was surrounded on all sides by thick woods. We were there for quite a while and when we got back into the truck to leave, I noticed that a little spider had spun a rather intricate little web from the window frame down to the mirror on my side of the truck. I didn't say anything, I just watched as we moved faster and faster down the road. The web began to tear and break against the force of the wind. Now, I don't even pretend to like spiders, but somehow this little guy fascinated me and I could not take my eyes off him. I was actually rooting for him, wanting him to leave his torn web and crawl to safety; to survive the terrible beating he was taking.

Bobbing and swirling in the wind, I was convinced he would go flying off at any moment but guess what? That little spider hung onto that single strand of web with all his might. It never broke but held him fast, and he hung on to it the whole twenty-minute drive back to our house. I couldn't help but think about it later and compare that single strand of web to Christ. I thought of how I felt like that little spider in a way, bobbing and swirling in the face of what felt to me certain destruction (the pain of my grief) but, instead holding fast to Christ, the Solid Rock, and not letting go for anything.

At that moment, I wondered if God watched me like I watched that spider; always mindful of what was going on. Would I hang on tight to His promises and weather the storm around me, or would I just give up and let go?

Don't misunderstand me, I had my dark days for sure but for every terrible day there was also a couple of good ones, a ray of light every now and again, and hope. I had to look for that and keep believing that relief would come and that someday, I would feel better. It IS hard work.

I remember one of those especially dark days one Sunday as we went to church. I'm not sure exactly how long Hunter had been gone by that time but, during the music and worship that morning, I began to cry and I could not stop. I just tried to mop up as best I could and keep my head down so maybe people around me wouldn't notice the black streaks running down my face!

All at once a young girl walked onto the stage with a guitar in her arms and began strumming the most beautiful melody. As she sang the song she herself had written, I recognized some of the lyrics as scripture verses I'd read before:

"When you pass through the waters, I will be with you;

and when you pass through the rivers, they will not sweep over you.

When you walk through the fire, you will not be burned; the flames will not set you ablaze." [6]

It was as if she was singing her beautiful song for no one else but me. I held on to that tune and those lyrics, and to this day, that precious song still comforts me. I would encourage you again to remember that most everyone goes to that pit of depression. The important thing is not to stay there and make it your permanent home. That is called getting 'stuck' in grief and that never does you any good or moves you toward healing. It takes a lot of courage to climb out and continue on.

One of the facilitators of our GriefShare group described it best when she told us, "Discard your 'rear view mirror'. Don't keep looking back all the time. Constantly looking to your past or to your image will impede your recovery. Like it or not, your life has changed and you will eventually have a *new* normal. Gain your strength from God and move ahead to a new normal." That doesn't mean that you can never remember — heavens, no! Just don't live in the "what was" or "what might have been" and don't let that loss become your identity.

Some people ask me about medications. I've already told you I am no doctor. There are certain circumstances where they can be very helpful; I think there is no doubt about that. I would just remind you that you can only medicate your grief for so long, but know you have to face it at some point. Sometimes, talking to others or journaling in private can be the best medicine for you.

I *can* tell you that tears are very healing. Don't be afraid to let them flow. Sometimes medications won't let that happen. Just remember that and use caution here. Seek wise and godly counsel that will help you back to a more stable place to deal and heal.

Earlier, I suggested journaling or writing a letter or series of letters. My husband, Eldon began journaling a year or so after Hunter's death. What he has shared with me in his journal has blessed my soul beyond belief. There are dreams he had about Hunter that he documented there, and he wrote down things he wanted to tell Hunter, like what a certain person did on a certain day and so forth. He reads those on occasion to the whole family when we're gathered and they make us all smile. As I mentioned before, it can be very helpful to read what you've journaled and see just how far you've come, how God has been at work in your life and so on. Remember, if you do journal, you don't have to share those writings with anyone. Sharing them with others is your prerogative.

Also, scrap booking or making photo albums can help lift your spirits and the rest of the family's as well. A time where everyone can look at pictures and reminisce can be a great and healing experience.

Walking in the woods or down by running streams or in some favorite place, enjoying God's creation and just getting some fresh air can be a wonderful thing, too.

Don't forget to take care of yourself. This is VERY important! Eat something nutritious, even when you don't feel hungry. Try to rest or take a little nap if you are able. I know it can be very difficult, but try. Talk to others; if not family members, then maybe a friend at your church or attend a group where there are others you can talk to that know about the pain. There will be those that love you and care about you but won't want to talk because they're afraid talking about your loved one will make you cry or feel worse. If that's the case, they might not talk to you at all but please understand, not everyone will feel comfortable talking about your loss. You will find people that will allow you to talk and will talk to you. It will be helpful and healing for you, and maybe them, too. Allow yourself those moments but remember, you are still here, still on that journey. Breathe deep and read these words slowly:

"When you pass through the waters,
I will be with you
When you pass through the rivers,
they will not overflow you
When you walk through the fire
you will not be scorched,
nor will the flame burn you

Do not fear for I have redeemed you
Do not fear for I have called you by name

You are mine, You are mine I have redeemed you

I am the Lord your God, The holy one of Israel,
I will say to the north give them up, I will say to
the south don't hold them back, bring my sons
and my daughters from afar.

Do not fear for I have redeemed you
Do not fear for I have called you by name"[7]

Those are the lyrics to the sweet song I heard that morning in church. I encourage you to find Kelly Jones Park's CD, "Do Not Fear," and listen to it. You will be blessed by that song and the rest of her music.

There might be people that throw scriptures at you like magic bullets and you know they mean well, but believe me when I say, I know that right now, you are probably not in a place where Romans 8:28 blesses your heart! God's Word is powerful and I would point you to the Psalms. There, you will find plenty of pain, confusion and crying out. You only need to look. I would encourage you to use these or find some of your own that speak directly to you. Write them down on little sticky notes or index cards and try taping them to your bathroom mirror, the dash of your car or in your closet. It's funny but you might open a cabinet door at the precise moment you need some encouragement and there it will be – a scripture for you to read. It really does work. I had a hard time reading my Bible for a while but, *when my heart was ready*, I did find some scriptures that really helped encourage me. I pray they touch you as well and remind you of the promise we have in HIM.

So do not fear, for I am with you; do not be dismayed, for I am your God. I will strengthen you and help you; I will uphold you with my righteous right hand. Isaiah 41:10

Because of the Lord's great love we are not consumed, for his compassions never fail. They are new every morning; great is your faithfulness. I say to myself, "The Lord is good to those whose hope is in him, to the one who seeks him". Lamentations 3:22-24.

Cast your cares on the Lord and he will sustain you; he will never let the righteous fall. Psalm 55:22

In the day of my trouble I will call to you, for you will answer me. Psalm 86:7

Do not let your hearts be troubled. Trust in God; trust also in me. In my Father's house are many rooms; if it were not so, I would have told you. I am going there to prepare a place for you. John 14:1-2

I have told you these things, so that in me you may have peace. In this world you will have trouble. But take heart! I have overcome the world. John 16:33

Praise be to the God and Father of our Lord Jesus Christ, the Father of compassion and the God of all comfort, who comforts us in all our troubles, so that we can comfort those in any trouble with the comfort we ourselves have received from God. II Corinthians 1:3-4

Do not be anxious about anything, but in everything, by prayer and petition, with thanksgiving, present your requests to God. And the peace of God, which transcends all understanding, will guard your hearts and your minds in Christ Jesus. Philippians 4:6-7

May our Lord Jesus Christ himself and God our Father, who loved us and by his grace gave us eternal encouragement and good hope, encourage your hearts and strengthen you in every good deed and word. II Thessalonians 2:16-17

Cast all your anxiety on him because he cares for you. I Peter 5:7

ACCEPTANCE~

This last one is my favorite I guess because I realized it was the real key to my freedom from the pain. I'd really rather call it PEACE. In fact, Greta and I were having a conversation one day about that very thing. I think it might have been one day when we went out to change the flowers on Hunter's grave.

As we both shared our different versions of our acceptance with Hunter's death, Greta looked at me, smiled that sweet smile of hers and said, "You know, I guess the thing that best describes it for me is the scripture that talks about the 'peace that passes all understanding.'[8]" I hadn't quite thought of it in that way but I agreed, "Yeah, that's it." When I got home, I looked it up, and then, another verse came to mind that fit perfectly for me as well – "Peace I leave with you, My peace I give you. I do not give to you as the world gives. Do not let your hearts be troubled and do not be afraid."[9] I felt like the Lord was telling me, "You know this feeling that you have now? The way you felt when you and Greta went to Hunter's grave today? Well, that's MY peace. I'm giving it to you now but I want you to realize that it's not like any other peace and it IS from Me."

I understand He wasn't telling me I couldn't ever be sad, I couldn't ever cry when I thought about Hunter or that I wouldn't miss him anymore. He was just reminding me that His peace is entirely different from the world's definition of peace.

Don't misunderstand me here – I still cry sometimes when I think about Hunter. I still miss him terribly and I still get "blue" on occasion but it never lasts long, because I know God's promises are true and I believe them with all my heart. It's easier now for me to refer to those verses because, for the most part, I've memorized them and hidden them in my heart.

Several months after hearing Kelly's wonderful song, I ran across a little insert that they put into our church bulletin every Sunday morning. It's called "Steps to Peace with God" and that word PEACE caught my eye right away. I realize that these "steps" are mostly for people that have never met

God and do not know His Son, Jesus. They are the all-important steps to salvation, but I wanted to share them with you here so you can reflect on them too.

STEPS TO PEACE WITH GOD[10]

STEP#1: God's Purpose: Peace and Life
John 10:10: "I have come that they may have life, and that they may have it more abundantly." Since God planned for us to have peace and abundant life right now, why are most people not having this experience?

STEP#2: Our Problem: Separation
God created us in His own image to have an abundant life. He did not make us as robots to automatically love and obey Him, but gave us a will and freedom of choice. We choose to disobey God and go our own willful way. We still make this choice today. This results in separation from God. The Bible says… "For the wages of sin is death, but the gift of God is eternal life in Christ Jesus our Lord." Romans 6:23. Our choice results in separation from God.

STEP#3: God's Remedy: The Cross
Jesus Christ is the only answer to this problem. He died on the Cross and rose from the grave, paying the penalty for our sin and bridging the gap between God and man. The Bible says…

"God is on one side and all the people on the other side, and Christ Jesus, Himself Man, is between them to bring them together..." I Timothy 2:5

STEP#4: Our Response: Receive Christ

We must trust Jesus Christ and receive Him by personal invitation. The Bible says "Behold, I stand at the door and knock. If anyone hears My voice and opens the door, I will come in to him, and he with Me." Revelation 3:20

"If you confess with your mouth the Lord Jesus and believe in your heart that God has raised Him from the dead, you will be saved." Romans 10:9. Is there any good reason why you cannot receive Jesus Christ right now?

What to pray: Dear Lord Jesus, I know that I am a sinner and need Your forgiveness. I believe that You died for my sins. I want to turn from my sins. I now invite You to come into my heart and life. I want to trust You as Savior and follow You as Lord, in the fellowship of Your church.

What caught my attention was Step# 1 and the question, "Since God planned for you to have abundant life..." That makes more sense to me now than ever before. Think about what you "orbit" around, what you think gives meaning to your life and brings you joy – your center. Many people might recite a list of answers like: my husband or wife, my kids, my job, my savings account, my hobbies, our house, my car, our boat; the list can go on and on. Most of those things can (and will) disappear. When they do, you can be knocked out of your "orbit", your comfort zone; peace and happiness are gone. God's peace isn't about creature comforts or possessions or even a certain set of circumstances. It's peace that "passes all understanding" and defies all human logic. It's heavenly, it's supernatural and it's available to us all, *especially* those of us in pain that know Him, no matter what.

If your center is your relationship with God, that can never be taken away. Did you get that? It can NEVER be taken away. The storms will come and they will batter us, bruise us, break our hearts and make us cry, but a personal relationship with the Lord is forever - eternal.

chapter six
God's Plan

After reading about hope in the previous chapters, maybe now you won't find it so hard to believe that I DID find peace after all that pain. I did make it through in one piece and you can too. You can't just snap your fingers and be all better. I wish it could be that way but it just can't. It is a process and it takes time, sometimes a very long time.

With all that said, I want to share some truly amazing things that happened *after* Hunter's death. These are the things that, along with God's promises to us, have kept us looking up and remembering there was a perfect plan for Hunter's life and for ours as well.

Remembering back to the day of the funeral was hard, and Chris and I talked several times about it while I was writing this book. We were both trying to remember exactly what went on that day at the service but, as you might imagine, our memories are still a bit sketchy. It was a very emotional service and some of it is still, to this day, a blur in my mind.

What I do remember is that, at the close of the service, Chris wanted to say something to the people gathered there. My son stood, took a microphone and looked out into the extremely large sea of faces. I watched his face as he spoke tenderly of his only son and how much he loved him. He said he knew that Hunter would have been thrilled to see all the big machines in the parking lot. (We were building onto our church and there were earthmovers and bulldozers everywhere. Those kinds of equipment were right up his alley!) Everyone chuckled a little.

Then, quite unintentionally but with such clarity of thought and passion, he began to preach one of the best evangelistic sermons I've ever heard. He told the crowd that, as they could plainly see, death *was* real and they should not doubt that God was real.

He talked about his pain and told them how hard it had been. He told that audience of people about the verse Hunter had recited to us the day he died and how it couldn't go unmentioned. He also confessed that he had told the Lord, "If just one person comes to know the love of Jesus Christ through this whole thing, it would be worth it." I know he had thought about it for a long time before he said it, because my Chris doesn't just blurt out things like that. Hearing those words, I began to cry.

Chris talked to that crowd for what seemed like an hour but I'm sure it was more like five minutes or so. He told them about the promise of Heaven and how certain he was that Hunter was already there. He told that large gathering of people that if any of them had any unfinished business (his words) with the Lord, they had better get it settled before they left the building that day because, as they could plainly see, none of us knew what the next minute held, let alone the next day.

It was very moving and there were many more tears. I was so proud of him for standing up and telling it how we all knew it was. But I was the proudest for Chris helping to make Hunter's death mean something, something important, encouraging those in attendance that day not to miss the greater meaning of it all. It was truly amazing to me and still, to this day, I cannot think back on that without many tears of pride and love for my son.

In the weeks and months that followed, we began to hear some amazing accounts of others whose lives Hunter had touched through the story of his death:

~ In a Fellowship of Christian Athletes meeting at a local junior high school, a coach had shared Hunter's story with the young men, comparing Chris losing his son to God sending HIS son to die for us. After the meeting, many of the young men came forward, desiring a deeper personal relationship with Christ.

~ We knew a young father that traveled frequently for his job and was rarely at home with his wife and baby daughter. Their marriage was strained because of his long absences. After hearing Hunter's story, he decided to find another job that would allow him to be home every night with his wife and child. He told us he realized that his family was much more important than any extra money he would make on the road away from them. We still talk to him occasionally and their marriage is healthy and their family is strong.

~ Chris' "cell group" of young men from our church that met regularly for Bible study, prayer and fellowship were so touched by Hunter's life and death (most of them knew him personally and played football with him at the house on numerous occasions) that they all signed a football and brought it to Chris at the funeral. These young men were greatly impacted to improve and strengthen their relationships with their Savior and years later, many of these guys have gone on to invest their lives in younger men and lead cell groups of their own.

~ I know a young man that told me he had been "straying" from his walk with the Lord and hadn't been living as he knew he should. He told me that after Hunter's death, he wanted his time to matter while he was here on this earth and he re-dedicated his life to Jesus Christ and began working with the youth in his church.

~ An acquaintance of ours told us that, when he heard of Hunter's death, he became very angry at God and subsequently tried to commit suicide. Thankfully, his attempt failed and he came out to our house to tell us about it, though still very depressed and despondent. Through his visit that day with Eldon, he gave his life to Jesus Christ. He was so impacted by the whole event that he built a garden fountain in Chris and Greta's front yard in Hunter's memory. We had a memorial service at that very same fountain one year later on the first anniversary of Hunter's death. We invited the police, fire and EMT's that had worked so hard to help us find Hunter that day and Chris & Greta presented them with plaques, thanking them for their brave service to the community and to our family.

~Immediately after the funeral, Eldon rented a cabin near Branson for the whole family to go and stay the weekend, just to get away together. We spent three days quietly reflecting, getting closer to our Lord and each other as a family. When the resort manager heard why we were there, she contacted us later to ask us if they could do something in Hunter's memory. The following spring a little dogwood tree was planted on the grounds with a small plaque beside it. Now, we all make the journey back every year to have our picture taken around the tree, documenting how our family, as well as how the little tree is changing and growing. That little tree always provides an opportunity for us to share his story, as well as the Good News of the Gospel of Christ with many strangers as we've stayed there over the years.

There are countless other stories I could tell you that I've heard since Hunter's death. Stories of people giving their hearts to Christ, re-committing their lives to Him, re-evaluating their priorities for themselves and their families; truly amazing stories of people who were touched by Hunter's story and thought enough of us to share with us. When Chris and Greta stopped counting, there were over fifty professions of faith in Christ as a direct result of hearing Hunter's story. I'm also sure that there were many things that happened we will never know about this side of Heaven but that's alright, I guess. Now, I think back to the day we all prayed before Hunter was ever born, over Greta's tummy, asking God to use that little life for His glory. He answered our prayer in a way we never expected!

Whenever I hear a new story or even remember some of the ones I already know, my mind goes back to that day at the funeral and Chris' words ring in my ears, "If just one person comes to know the Lord through this thing, then I will have to say it was worth it." Those words weren't used flippantly or in haste but spoken in all truth and honesty by a young man that loved his only son with his whole heart. A young man that wanted people to know Hunter's life wasn't in vain and his death wasn't just some random tragedy that we would never understand.

I want to tell you that the person you're grieving over right now, the person you've lost – their life wasn't in vain either. You must celebrate their life and realize it did count for something, no matter how young or old they were. You must have HOPE and FAITH in Christ. Faith in the truth that God has a plan and it's bigger than just you or me or what we can see with our eyes or understand with our minds. You may not be able to count the blessings in your situation yet, but believe that there is a purpose and, who knows, you may even hear stories like these soon, too.

Sometimes, as we've seen earlier, it takes a while to get to that place. I just want you to know that God loves you and He knows about your pain. Remember, He felt that pain too when His only son, Jesus, died on the cross **FOR YOU**! And He too said, "If only one person comes to know My son, Jesus as their personal Savior, then it's worth it."

Don't ever doubt that He has a plan for your life. Begin to talk with Him about just what that plan might be and then do your best to begin to follow it. Journal about it. Find someone willing to listen to you and talk to them openly and honestly. Tell them what you're feeling.

If you can't find someone to talk to right now, keep talking to God. He knows your circumstances and He *can* meet your needs all by Himself. I would strongly encourage you to find someone you can trust to talk with; someone who might be considered "godly counsel." Look in the yellow pages for a local church or google 'GriefShare' for a group meeting in your area. Get with them and share.

Vow to honor your loved one by making a positive change in your life or the lives of others. Work through it as only you can but never, never, NEVER give up and never give in. Keep trusting God, even when (or especially when) you don't know how. Peace will come, but remember; it's not *earned or bargained for.* It's given by God's wonderful grace as a result of our faith and trust in Him.

I pray blessings to you on your journey and leave you with these wonderful words of triumphant faith found in Psalm 27:13-14.

"I am still confident of this: I will see the goodness of the Lord in the land of the living. Wait for the Lord; be strong and take heart and wait for the Lord."

Postscript: Greta has since given birth to Samuel Ryker Long in August of 2008 and Jordan Nathaniel Long in December of 2010 (Hunter's little brothers). Our youngest daughter, CeCe and her husband, Dustin (who had Jackson McKenzie in April of 2005) gave us another little boy, Jaden Dustin Long, born just six days after Samuel in 2008. Our oldest daughter and middle child, Casey and her husband, Pete, had a baby girl in December of 2008: Miss Aubrey Abigail Reynolds!

"You have turned my mourning into joyful dancing. You have taken away my clothes of mourning and clothed me with joy, that I might sing praises to You and not be silent. O Lord my God, I will give you thanks forever!" Psalm 30:11-12.

acknowledgements

There are so many people that have supported and loved me through the writing of this book. I
may have left some out by accident and I apologize
but please know I love you all dearly.

Eldon, my beloved husband of forty years:
Your love and wisdom amazes me and I continue to
thank the Lord for every day we have together and
your untiring support.

Chris, my only son: You are the inspiration
for me every single day, Sweetheart. No words could
ever be written in any book to make you understand
how much I love you. I am so proud of the godly
man you are.

Greta, my daughter-in-love: How I love you
and what an example of Christ's love you are to
everyone you meet! These two new miracles of
God's love, Samuel and Jordan are a testimony
of your faithfulness to Him.

Casey and CeCe, my beautiful daughters:
You have loved and supported me in this and I love
you for that. I know remembering was hard for you.
I love you both so much for the women you are and
the wonderful mothers you have become. Girls, you
know you are a precious *double blessing* to me.

Our Fellowship family: Always loving,
gently leading and pointing us to the Savior. Thank
you for being there, counseling and praying for us
and with us.

Tom and Jan Stockdale: You led our
family through the most difficult of times, boldly
exemplifying the love of Christ to us. Your love,

understanding and endless compassion is beyond compare.

My "Apples of Gold" (ladies Bible study group): Thank you for listening, laughing and crying with me. You girls are my biggest cheering section.

Carie (and Andrew): We will always have that tie between us that few share, and… thanks for keeping me on track.

The Burrell family, our neighbors: More tender hearts I have never known. How we love your sweet family.

Brad, Paul, Aaron and everyone at the station: I thank God every day for the relationships we've formed because of Hunter. I love you guys.

Montana: Thank you for being Hunter's best buddy.

Marjorie Wolfe & Jennie Younkin: Thank you for walking with us on our journey and teaching us how to grieve in a healthy way. Love you so much!

footnotes/references

1. E. Kubler-Ross,
    On Death and Dying (New York: MacMillan, 1969),
    pg. 34-121

2. "Footprints in the Sand"
    poem by Mary Stevenson, 1936

3. "GriefShare,
    Grief Recovery Support Groups,"
    griefshare.org

4. Webster's New World Dictionary, 2nd Edition
    (New York: Hungry Minds, Inc., 2002),
    pg. 166

5. Thomas O. Chisholm and William M. Runyan,
    "Great Is Thy Faithfulness", 1923

6. Isaiah 43:2.

7. Kelly Jones Parks,
    "You Are Mine",
    Do Not Fear, 2001

8. Philippians 4:7

9. John 14:27

10. Billy Graham Evangelistic Association,
    "Steps To Peace With God",
    billygraham.org/articlepage.asp?articleid=470

CPSIA information can be obtained
at www.ICGtesting.com
Printed in the USA
LVHW012246181021
700802LV00003B/62